INTRODUCTION

Some people think the main task of Christianity is to give people answers to life's questions. But that's not entirely the way of Jesus. In fact, Jesus often seems to do the exact opposite: asking difficult questions about life's purpose, end, and meaning.

The gospels have important teaching moments; for example, Matthew presents Jesus as a teacher and records five large sections of his instruction, the most famous being the Sermon on the Mount. However, we easily overlook the curious fact that Jesus asked questions in the gospels, lots of them. I was surprised some years ago by the book "The questions of Jesus" by John Dear. I looked it over and thought – did Jesus ask enough questions to warrant an entire book on the subject?

I was astonished by the book's introduction, which stated that Jesus asked over 300 questions of people in the gospels. It seemed that in every situation, Jesus had a specific and probing question. Dear writes, "The gospels are filled with stories, actions, parables, miracles, commandments, declarations, imperatives, and incidents from the dramatic life of Jesus. But they are also filled with questions. Jesus has a question for everyone he meets, for every occasion, for every experience, for every potential disciple. From his first encounter with his future disciples to his last words before his ascension, Jesus looks at his friends and invites them deeper into the mystery of God by means of a probing question."

For a time, I worked with university students on a public campus in Canada. While I was doing that work, I created a ministry called "tea time" where students would gather twice a week to drink tea and discuss current issues, world news and ideas. Over the course of a few months, I began to notice something that seemed a bit troubling. Every time an issue would come up, the majority of the students around the table would quickly state with certainty what they thought the correct answer was, especially with issues and ideas around religion. It seemed to me that many of these students were nurtured in a religious culture that encouraged *answer giving* rather than *question asking*.

In an attempt to challenge this behavior and encourage humility, honesty and open-mindedness, I began to work with the leadership team of students in a way that would free them to become curious and seekers on a journey. Taking John Dear's book off the shelf, I began paging through it again (after many years) and I thought that maybe the questions of Jesus would be a good place to start. I wrote down the top 23 questions that I thought would speak to university students, cut the individual questions into strips and put them into a hat. Our leadership team prayed, asking God to give each of us a question of Jesus that would speak into our lives. With holy anticipation mixed with a dash of trepidation, each person reached into the hat and pulled out a question. Each student reverently opened the creased paper and read the question out loud; ancient and probing questions like these began to be ring around that small room: Who do you say that I am? (Mark 8:29) What is it you want? (Matthew 20:21) Why are you so afraid? Do you still have no faith? (Mark 4:40) If I am telling the truth, why do you not believe me? (John 8:46) Why do you call me Lord, Lord – and not do what I tell you? (Luke 6:46) Will you really lay down your life for me? (John 13:38) Do you love me? (John 21:16). I then challenged the students to read the question in its original context and to reflect on it with the help of this guiding question: Why this question for me this week?

I was surprised at how seriously the students engaged this exercise. Spontaneous conversations erupted in doorways and hallways that week as students wrestled with the difficult questions of Jesus. I assured them that the important thing was that they begin wrestling towards an authentic response to Jesus rather than having a watertight and "correct" answer. When we gathered together as a group again, students began pulling their little pieces of crinkled and worn paper from wallets, pockets, purses, journals and bibles. They opened them, reminding the group which question they had received and began sharing how the question led them on a journey of discovery, confusion, questioning, probing, seeking and prayer. Most of the students could express how the question and their particular life circumstances were intersecting and indicated how they felt their question was "meant" for them. One student in particular had a break through moment that week and spent significant time in her dorm room crying because she was so humbled by the way God was speaking into her life through the question that she had pulled out of the hat: "do you understand what I have done for you?" (John 13:12) This particular question was one more confirmation among many over the past few months that God was speaking to her and working in her heart.

The Jesus Questions are now a regular part of the ministry that I do. And, to my surprise, the people that I work with eagerly look forward to it. It seems to me that we all need someone to give us permission to be seekers on a journey of discovery. To become "answer - seekers" rather than "answer - givers."

May God give us all the courage and grace to discover our authentic answers to the probing, difficult and encouraging questions of Jesus.

God bless!

Sam Gutierrez

INSTRUCTIONS

The Jesus Questions is a participatory study for all ages that helps people engage and ponder the questions of Jesus. Twenty-three of the most poignant questions that Jesus asked in the gospels are put into a container. The questions are prayed over and each person draws one question out of the container to reflect on for the week. During the week, participants are encouraged to dive into the Bible to understand the original context for the question they received. They are also encouraged to explore what Jesus is saying to them personally through the question. Participants are challenged to journal about their question and to engage friends, family, and non-christians in reflection upon their question. The following week, participants gather to share their thoughts, questions, answers, struggles, and ideas. Then, all the questions go back into the container and they choose another question for the next week.

The whole process then repeats for as many times as the group desires. However, I have found that a four-week study is a good amount of time. During these four weeks, three questions are drawn (the last week, there is only sharing and no new question.) Because the questions of Jesus are so challenging, it is better to do a four-week study, and then maybe come back to it after a few months of studying something else.

The Jesus Questions is relatively simple to plan and lead, but highly participatory and challenging. It engages people of all ages and encourages all participants to become seekers on a journey of authentic response rather than theological answer-givers. The Jesus Questions can be adapted for a weekend retreat or expanded for a Lenten study/series. It can be implemented in small groups or as a sermon series with the whole congregation. The leader is not an answer giver but a guide on the journey. The group functions well when everyone participates and brings something to share with the whole group. Everyone is valued and everyone has something of value to contribute.

OTHER WAYS TO ENGAGE THE STUDY

Retreat ~ Weekend retreat (condense the study) 2-3 days

Lent ~ Lent Experience (expand the study) 7 weeks

Sermon Series ~ 4 week sermon series. Someone draws a question during the service, the whole community reflections on it during the week and the preacher preaches on that passage/question the following Sunday.

WAYS TO DEEPEN THE EXPERIENCE

Personal Prayers of Desire ~ Take a small piece of paper. Write a short prayer to God on one side that engages with this question - what do you desire to happen through this 4 week experience? Write your name on the other side. Tape the paper to a container (which holds the questions) with the prayer facing the inside – the name facing the outside. At the end of 4 weeks, take the prayer off and discover how God answered your prayer. Share with the group.

Spiritual Companion ~ Find a spiritual companion for the journey. Call or meet midweek to encourage, share and reflect. Works best if the spiritual companion is someone who is also participating in the Jesus Questions.

Meal Time Devotions ~ Read the passage from which the question comes every night for devotions. Talk about it as a family.

Mission ~ Use the question as a way to engage others (friends, family, neighbors, coworkers) in spiritual discussions. Say – I'm reflecting on this question of Jesus this week and then simply ask – what do you think it means?

HOW TO HEAR JESUS

When I was in seminary, we took a class called "Old Testament narratives." The class was broken into 3 groups and we were all given the same Old Testament passage to study, memorize and deliver to the class in dramatic fashion. Most of the staging was rather simple - roles were chosen, positions were practiced and a limited number of props were fashioned or found. However, what wasn't simple was trying to figure out how to deliver God's speaking parts. When God speaks, what does he sound like? Does he whisper or shout? Is his tone condescending, sarcastic, gentle, commanding, sympathetic, frustrated, confident, patient or playful?

If you receive a question like, *"Why are you so afraid?"* (Mark 4:40) - how do you "hear" it? What is the volume, tone, and inflection? Is Jesus's sad? Disappointed? Frustrated? Angry? Some people hear Jesus that way. How we hear the question reveals something about our image of God. Try reading the question with a humous and encouraging tone. Is it possible that Jesus is smiling as he speaks those words? Is there a sparkle in his eye and playfulness in his voice as he invites us deeper into the mystery of his grace and love? That approach too reveals something about our image of God.

I encourage you to be aware of not only the question during this experience, but how it's being asked. The Jesus Questions expose our image of God and often, that image is a mixture of our mom, dad, teacher, pastor, aunt, uncle, brother or sister. So, if you're feeling a bit lost and the only tone you hear as you ponder a question of Jesus is an angry, frustrated, accusing or condescending one, then I want to remind you that God is love and love is patient and kind. Read the question using the "tone" of each of the descriptors found in 1 Corinthians 13 ~

1 Corinthians 13

Love is patient,
love is kind.
It does not envy,
it does not boast,
it is not proud.

It does not dishonor others,
it is not self-seeking,
it is not easily angered,
it keeps no record of wrongs.

Love does not delight in evil
but rejoices with the truth.

It always protects,
always trusts,
always hopes,
always perseveres.

Love never fails.

THE JESUS QUESTIONS
Taken from the New International Version (NIV)

Why are you so afraid?
Mark 4:40

What do you want me to do for you?
Mark 10:36

Who do people say that I am?
Mark 8:27

Who do you say that I am?
Mark 8:29

Do you want to be well?
John 5:6

Do you believe that I am able to do this?
Matthew 9:28

Why are you troubled?
Luke 24:38

Why do doubts arise in your mind?
Luke 24:38

What do you want?
John 1:38

Do you understand what I have done for you?
John 13:12

Why do you call me Lord, Lord and do not do what I say?
Luke 6:46

Will you really lay down your life for me?
John 13:38

What good is it for someone to gain the whole world, yet forfeit their soul?
Mark 8:36

Why do you look at the speck of sawdust in your brother's eye, and pay no attention to the plank in your own eye?
Matthew 7:3-4

Who is it you want?
John 18:4,7

Why were you searching for me?
Luke 2:49

Do you love me more than these?
John 21:15

Do you love me?
John 21:16

Who of you by being worrying can add a single hour to your life?
Luke 12:25

Why do you entertain evil thoughts in your hearts?
Matthew 9:4

If you love those who love you, what reward will you get?
Matthew 5:46

If I am telling the truth, why don't you believe me?
John 8:46

Do you still have no faith?
Mark 4:40

THE JESUS QUESTIONS PRAYER

Spend a few moments in silence. Then, say this prayer together as a group. Next, pass the container around. Each person will draw a question, read it out loud and pass the container to the next person.

Father, Son and Holy Spirit,

Direct our hands. Guide our fingers. As we choose a question, we ask that you choose one for each one of us. Speak to us Lord, and give us a question that will challenge, unnerve, transform, realign, and encourage.

Empower us to become seekers and send us on a journey to discover authentic answers to your probing questions. May your Spirit illuminate our minds, open our hearts and ready our bodies to hear, see, wrestle, reflect, and answer honestly without fear of you, Lord or judgement from others.

We pray this in the name of Jesus,

Amen.

Q ~ Who do you say I am? *Mark 8:29*

Short Reflection
At this point, what others are saying about Jesus fades away. Jesus turns to you and asks you personally. Try speaking the name that naturally arises out of your heart.

Discussion Prompts
Reflect for a few minutes on your life and consider how God has been present to you. After reflecting, what is your response to this question in light of your experience of God?

Are you surprised by your answer? Why or why not?

Prayer
God, there are many names that describe who you are. Today, I speak out of my experience and use the name _____ to begin this conversation with you...

Digging Deeper
Search the book of Mark and make a list of the names that people call Jesus. Look over the list. What questions arise for you out of the list? Which ones do you resonate with? Which seem strange or foreign to you.

This conversation and question comes at the midpoint of Mark's gospel. What was Mark's intention? What does it mean for you?

Immediately before this question, Mark tells a story about someone who experiences various stages of blindness and sight. Why does Mark put this story right before the conversation about the identity of Jesus?

Q ~ **Do you love me?** *John 21:16*

Reflection
Picture yourself on the beach. You are one of his disciples. Jesus turns to you and asks - Do you love me? In your imagination, look into the eyes of Jesus as he asks the question. Eyes are a window to the soul. They give us insight into the inner life of a person. What do you see in the eyes of Jesus?

Discussion Prompts
Peter was hurt when Jesus asked him a third time. If Jesus asked you three times, how do you think you'd feel? Why?

Have you ever been loved deeply or loved someone else deeply? What was that experience like? Can you put it into words?

Prayer
Jesus, you ask such demanding and difficult questions. You ask me to be vulnerable, sensitive and open - which is sometimes hard and scary. You also encourage me to be honest. My honest answer to your question is...   The reason for that is because...

Digging Deeper
Jesus could have asked Peter - Will you deny me again? Can I trust you? But instead, Jesus asks Peter - Do you love me? Why?

Why do you think Jesus asked Peter such a personal question in front of the other disciples instead of pulling him off to the side to have a private conversation?

After Peter's response, Jesus says that Peter will die for that love. What are the connections between love and dying?

Q ~ **What do you want me to do for you?** *Mark 10:36*

Reflection
In this passage, we encounter a God who is generous and who wants to hear our requests and even grant them. It's comforting to know that we can come to Jesus just as we are without fear of judgment from him. Sometimes the things we want are not good for us or good for those around us. We have to trust that Jesus knows our hearts and will answer our prayers according to his goodness, wisdom and glory.

Discussion Prompts
What is the difference between wants and needs? Does Jesus sometimes grant us the things we not only need, but want?

If you could ask Jesus for anything and you know it would be granted without question, what would you ask for? Why?

Prayer
Jesus, thank you for being open to my request(s). With boldness, I speak honestly the desires that are on my heart, no matter how right or wrong they may be. I trust that you want the best for me and will answer my prayer accordingly. I acknowledge that my understanding is severely limited and that yours is not.

Digging Deeper
When the other disciples heard what James and John asked of Jesus they were upset. Do you think the people you know would be upset if they knew your true desires?

Are you ever afraid to say what you really want? Why or why not? When is the last time you got in touch with your true dreams, desires, hopes and passions?

Jesus uses James and John's request to teach them an important lesson about leadership. In light of what you know about the Kingdom, take an objective view of your request (as if someone else had asked it). What lesson would Jesus teach you about the Kingdom after hearing your request?

Q ~ **Who do people say that I am?** *Mark 8:27*

Reflection
While on the road, Jesus wanted to hear the gossip about what others were saying about him. So he invited his disciples to spill the beans. They answered with three main descriptors - John the Baptist, Elijah, or one of the prophets. As to be expected, there are about as many opinions of Jesus as there are people in the world.

Discussion Prompts
What is the most common description of Jesus that you've heard throughout your life?

Are some descriptions of Jesus closer to the truth than others?

Prayer
Jesus, there is a lot of confusion out there about who you really are. To be honest, the confusion isn't just "out there..." - it's in my heart too. Sometimes I believe so strongly and other times my doubt is just as strong. In my times of belief, Lord give me humility and in my times of doubt, grant me your courage. Help me to see more clearly your true identity. Help me to share with others with patience and gentleness.

Digging Deeper
Why is there so much confusion (past and present) about the true identity of Jesus?

Before this story is a story about blindness and sight. What does blindness and sight have to do knowing the truth about Jesus. Can people know the truth without the Holy Spirit opening their eyes?

Do you think that all people, though they may deny it, know deep deep down that Jesus is truly the Son of God?

Q ~ **Why are you so afraid?** *Mark 4:40*

Reflection
The fear that the disciples experienced was not imaginary. There was a real possibility that they would drown. Jesus is asleep in the boat as the wind and the waves tossed the small boat back and forth. Shouldn't Jesus be more concerned?

Discussion Prompts
What role has fear played in your life. How do you know when you are afraid?

Do you know anyone who seems to be fearless? What lessons can you learn from them?

Prayer
Jesus, when things are bad, it's easy to question whether or not you care. It's easy to see the wind and the waves and to forget that you're in the boat. Jesus, wake up and help me. I want to trust you and to cast fear overboard, but I'm not there yet. Wake up Jesus and tame this terrible storm that threatens to swallow me whole. Jesus, I'm scared.

Digging Deeper
Make a list of what you are afraid of. Invite Jesus to speak his commanding voice - "Peace, be still" into those things.

Invite some friends over for tea. Share how fear has taken root in your lives. Pray for each other.

Imagine yourself in the boat. As the waves and wind threaten, watch Jesus sleeping. Resist the temptation to wake him up with your fear and panic. Instead, lay next to Jesus and allow yourself to rest. Close your eyes and place your hand on his chest. Breath slowly and deeply.

Q ~ **Do you want to be well?** *John 5:6*

Reflection
Jesus' question to the paralyzed man seems odd. The answer is obvious, isn't it? Of course the paralyzed man wants to be well... but does he? We learn that he has been paralyzed for 38 years. Sometimes being sick can become our "normal" way of operating. Sickness can become part of our identity. Sometimes we say we want to be well, but we really don't.

Discussion Prompts
Are the man's reasons for struggling to get into the pool legit or are they excuses?

The man said, "I have no one to help me..." What role do other people play in the healing process? When does helping become enabling?

Prayer
Jesus, I've been unhealthy for so long, that I've gotten used to it. It feels normal to me now. Give me insight into the areas of my life that are diseased and not working the way you intend. I have to admit that I've become content to live in a way that less than 100%. It's because I'm...   Ready my heart Lord, to be healed so that I may stand tall and walk in hope.

Digging Deeper
Do you want to be well? Why or why not? What are your reasons either way?

Is there a sickness that you've been carrying for a long time? How long? How have you been shaped by it?

Invite a friend out for coffee. Tell that friend about an area of your life that is diseased. Seek their counsel. Ask for prayer.

Q ~ **Do you believe that I am able to do this?** *Matthew 9:28*

Reflection
This is a simple story about two blind men who pursue Jesus calling out "Have mercy on us, Son of David." The title they use for Jesus here is important - they identify Jesus as the promised Messiah in the line of David. Jesus asks a poignant question, "do you believe I am able to do this." The two men have not asked for healing, but for mercy. Therefore what Jesus is asking is whether or not they believe he is able to show them mercy. Mercy flows from Jesus in the form of physical healing.

Discussion Prompts
We don't hear the word "mercy" much in our everyday vocabulary. What does mercy mean?

These two men are blind, but are able to see Jesus clearly. Discuss what it means to "see" clearly with the heart?

Prayer
Jesus, when our bodies don't work the way they are supposed to, it's terribly frustrating. You offer mercy, which sometimes takes the form of physical healing. Help me to desire mercy in whatever form it takes. It's easy to believe you are "able" - it's another matter altogether to believe that you are "willing." Give me the faith to believe that you are both. Give me grace to receive and celebrate your mercy when it does not take the form of physical healing.

Digging Deeper
What does it mean that God is mercy-full? Picture God full of mercy. What do you see?

Why do you think the two blind men asked for mercy instead of physical healing?

Petition God, letting him know that you believe He is "able." Then, pour out your heart asking God to act.

Q ~ **Why are you troubled?** *Luke 24:38*

Reflection
In this post resurrection story, Jesus appears to his disciples. The disciples think they are seeing a ghost. They are startled and scared. Jesus reassures them by showing them his hands and his feet. Then he invites them to touch him and experience his "realness."

Discussion Prompts
What is troubling you right now?

Why might gazing upon the crucified/resurrected feet and hands of Jesus be the cure for troubled hearts and minds?

Prayer
*Lord, I am surrounded by trouble. I feel scared. There is so much that is out of my control and I feeling anxious and worried. Give me the gift of experiencing you in a concrete way because sometimes you feel like a ghost to me. I know you exist, but I wonder if you can make a real difference in this messed up world. Come to me Jesus and let me not only see, but **feel** your hands and feet.*

Digging Deeper
The Bible is full of troubled people and troubling situations. Can you identify with a particular story or person?

Make a list of your troubles. Meet with a friend and pray together over each concern, placing it into the nailed scarred hands of Jesus.

Jesus wants you to tell him what has your heart so stirred up with worry. Hold nothing back. In your imagination, sit with Jesus. After you've poured out your troubles, place your hand in his crucified/resurrected hand. Hold hands for a while and sit in the silence.

Q ~ **Why do doubts arise in your mind(s)?** *Luke 24:38*

Reflection
When Jesus appeared to the disciples after the resurrection, they were filled with doubt. They couldn't believe that it was really Him. He came to them in a resurrected body, with resurrection power. It wasn't the same Jesus they remembered.

Discussion Prompts
What doubts to you have? Have you ever voiced them? Why or why not?

Why might gazing upon the crucified/resurrected feet and hands of Jesus be the cure for troubled hearts and minds?

Prayer
Jesus, people who have no doubts about their faith or about your goodness seem a bit suspect to me. There is so much in this world that calls into question your love, power and involvement. Thank you for taking my doubts seriously. Thank you for not being angry with me because I have doubts. Give me the strength and conviction to trust you without having to have all the answers to everything.

Digging Deeper
Make a list of your doubts. Are some more concerning/serious than others?

Rather than being afraid of your doubts, make friends with them. See them as companions on the journey. What helpful lessons are your doubts teaching you? What dangers are your doubts alerting you to?

The risen Jesus asks the question about doubts using the word "arise." What is the significance of this? How do doubts rise? From where do they rise? Where does their power come from?

Q ~ **What do you want?** *John 1:38*

Reflection
The questions of Jesus get at the deepest desires of our hearts. Jesus turns and asks the two who are following him this simple yet penetrating question.

Discussion Prompts
This is the first question that Jesus asks in the book of John. What is the significance of this?

Sometimes we feel more strongly about what we don't want. Why is it easier to know and share what we don't want rather than what we want?

Prayer
Jesus, sometimes I know what I want so clearly. Sometimes I feel confused and lost. Sometimes I'm afraid to acknowledge what I really want because it's just too painful. In reality, I want lots of things... but I hear your challenge to discover and name the WANT underneath the wants. It's hard work. Give me the tools, the support and the strength to dig deep.

Digging Deeper
The two men following Jesus wanted to know where Jesus was staying. They wanted to abide with him... to be with him. Where is Jesus right now?

They spent the day with Jesus. What do you think they did? What did they talk about? Try to get away for a day and spend it with Jesus. Meet a friend for coffee and share what it was like.

Is your deepest desire to dwell with Jesus? Why or why not.

Q ~ Do you understand what I have done for you? *John 13:12*

Reflection
Jesus washes his disciples feet, returns to his place around the table and puts on his robe. Then he asks the disciples this profound question. It extends beyond the upper room to include the manger, the cross and the empty tomb. It can even be taken back to the creation story in Genesis.

Discussion Prompts
What is relationship between, power, leadership, identity and service?

What is the modern equivalent of washing feet?

Prayer
*Jesus, at times I catch a glimpse of what you have done for me. But to say that I **understand** would be a lie. Thankfully, all it takes is a small glimpse to change my life forever and to live for you completely. One day I will understand fully all you have done, but until then transform me into a disciple seeking deepening levels of understanding. Open my heart, mind, ears and eyes. As you do, may I respond with equal amounts love and gratitude.*

Digging Deeper
Think of three specific things that God has done for you. Praise him. Then tell someone about God's goodness in your life.

A fitting response to God's generosity and goodness is gratitude. Hold a small "thanksgiving" gathering in the spring or summer. Have special food/dessert/drink and share together what you are thankful for.

Rather than speaking your thanks, try to feel it. Don't give up until you feel gratitude stirring in your heart. What does it feel like? When is the last time you felt **deep** gratitude?

Q ~ Why do you call me Lord, Lord and do not do what I say?
Luke 6:46

Reflection
This question comes at the end of the sermon on the mount. It's fairly easy to say "Lord, Lord." The story from which the question comes is a warning about the discrepancy between words and actions.

Discussion Prompts
How close do your words and actions line up?

Take an honest assessment of your life. Based on your life alone (not your words), who is your Lord?

Prayer
Jesus, your question exposes the hypocrite that I am. I admit that I pick and choose certain teachings to implement in my life... usually the least painful and inconvenient ones. My actions and my words are often out of sync, but sometimes they do line up and for that I thank you. Your grace and power is at work in my life. Thank you for this question... it hurts, but the honesty and humility it produces are freeing.

Digging Deeper
Go back over the sermon on the mount. (Matthew 5) Identify one thing that Jesus said that you are not currently putting into practice. Why?

What would happen if you tried to put the sermon on the mount into practice. What would you life look like? How would people know?

Think about someone you know who has built their life on a firm foundation. Now think of someone who has built their life on sand. Meditate on this.

Q ~ **Will you really lay down your life for me?** *John 13:38*

Reflection
Peter boldly proclaimed that he would lay down his life for Jesus. Jesus knows Peter better than Peter knows himself. Peter will one day be ready to really lay down his life for Jesus, but he has a lot of growing to do first. Rather than dying for Jesus, he will deny Jesus in a matter of hours. It's a humbling prediction.

Discussion Prompts
What does it mean to live for Jesus and die for Jesus at the same time?

Peter didn't know himself very well. How well do you know yourself? How far are you willing to go to follow Jesus?

Prayer
Jesus, you only ask of me what you yourself are willing to do. I know that you are willing to lay down your life for me, because you did. Help me to lay down my life for you in the small and ordinary circumstances of my life. Forgive me for the small and big ways I deny you everyday. You are so faithful to me Lord. Thank you for not giving up on me.

Digging Deeper
What aspect of your life are you holding to tightly, refusing to let it go? What would happen if you let it go and gave it over to Jesus?

Why is dying so scary?

Imagine yourself around that fire with Peter. When you hear the rooster crow, watch Peter's face. What do you see? How do you feel?

Q ~ What good is it for someone to gain the whole world, yet forfeit their soul? *Mark 8:36*

Reflection

Gaining possessions, status, likes, followers, degrees, property, information and experiences is more possible than ever before. Yet, Jesus spoke this question two thousand years ago. In this passage he makes a connection between gaining and losing - in this case gaining the "world" while losing the "soul." Jesus is a master teacher and lays before us what is at stake in this life.

Discussion Prompts

What is "soul?"

Is it possible to gain and not forfeit the soul?

Prayer

Jesus, thank you this question. It helps me to realize that I do things everyday that feed my ego rather than my soul. Help me to live in a more soul - full way and help me to see through the foolishness of running after things that don't last. Impress upon me the worth and value of the soul and then give me a single minded passion to seek your kingdom, losing my life for your sake.

Digging Deeper

What would the world look like if people paid more attention to the soul?

What makes your soul happy? What sucks your soul dry? What numbs your soul? What makes your soul want to dance?

Search out a friend and commit individually to do something that feeds/nurtures your soul this week. Then get together for coffee and talk about your experience.

Q ~ Why do you look at the speck of sawdust in your brother's eye and pay no attention to the plank in your own eye.
Mark 8:36

Reflection
Jesus uses an exaggerated and humours picture to describe how the judging scenario often plays out. His question is an honest one inviting us to dig deep into our hearts to gain understanding into *why* we judge others while ignoring our own obvious faults.

Discussion Prompts
Why is it easier to see other people's faults rather than our own?

Humbly share with the group the "plank(s)" in your eye.

Prayer
Oh Lord, free me from the need to judge others. I can be a harsh critic sometimes. You alone see clearly enough to judge. Not only that, you're a gracious and merciful judge - way more merciful than I am with others and sadly... myself. Help me to leave the judging up to you. As I journey with fellow pilgrims, give me the wisdom and humility to help others walk with increasing amounts of courage, faith and joy.

Digging Deeper
How do you balance accountability and speaking honestly to other believers without judging them?

How does judging others create a shaky foundation on which to build your life? (see Matt 7:24 - 27)

This will be hard to do, but ask a friend to tell you some of your "growth areas." Ask the Lord for the grace to humbly laugh at your shortcomings and thank your friend for loving you enough to tell you the truth.

Q ~ **Who is it you want?** *John 18:4,7*

Reflection
A mob consisting of soldiers, religious officials and a disciple -
Judas, came to the garden seeking Jesus.   Jesus asks them the
question above. They answer clearly - Jesus of Nazareth.

Discussion Prompts
Why does Jesus ask this question twice?

They went to seek Jesus at night. Why?

Prayer
*Jesus, You're a mystery to me sometimes. I pray that when you ask
me this question, I can answer quickly and with conviction - **You**.
Give me the passion to seek the REAL you and not the Jesus that I
or others have fashioned.*

Digging Deeper
The soldiers and officials said they were seeking "Jesus - of
Nazareth." Of all the names Jesus is called in the gospels, they
chose this one. Why?

Imagine yourself coming to Jesus, surrounded by friends,
coworkers, and family. Jesus asks you this question. In front of
everyone, what is your answer?

What does the night time have to do with seeking and with
identity?

Q ~ **Why were you searching for me?** *Luke 2:49*

Reflection
As a young boy, Jesus asks his parents and those looking for him this interesting question. We have lots of reasons why we search for Jesus. Sometimes at the root of our faith is fear. We don't want to go to hell. Sometimes we pray and seek God because we want him to bless us with materials possessions, good fortune, or good feelings.

Discussion Prompts
Why do we have to search for Jesus?

Is it possible to search for Jesus and not find him?

Prayer
Jesus, I seek you. But when I find you, you ask me this penetrating question about my motivation for seeking you in the first place. I know you're not a magic genie or a dispenser of good feelings or a way to minimize my fearful and anxious thoughts. Eventually, I want to seek you for LOVE alone, but I'm not sure I'm there yet. Purify my desire and give me the clarity to see that only love will enable to find and know you as you truly are.

Digging Deeper
Mary and Joseph were searching for the young Jesus because they loved him and were concerned for his health and safety. What are your reasons for seeking Jesus?

Inquire of others their motivations for seeking Jesus. What do you discover?

They searched 3 days before they found Jesus. What is the symbolic significance of this?

Q ~ **Do you love me more than these?** *John 21:15*

Reflection
The first question that Jesus asked Peter on the beach is this one. Later, Jesus drops the "these" part of the question and asks simply "Do you love me?" It's easy to think that maybe Jesus is just changing his question slightly to keep it fresh, but no word or phrase of Jesus is ever wasted. Jesus is purposeful when he asks this variation of the question.

Discussion Prompts
What or who are "these?"

Jesus is exposing that we have other "loves." The key to his question is whether or not we love Jesus "more." If you could make a list of your top "loves" - what/who would make the list?

Prayer
Jesus, my heart gets all mixed up and my various loves get disordered. Other things and people move up the list and sit in first place. Only you Lord, deserve to be my number one love. Nothing or No-one else is worthy. Reorder my loves, Lord. I surrender to you.

Digging Deeper
Was there ever a time in your life when Jesus was your number one love? Is that still the case? Why or why not?

Take an honest look at your actions rather than your words. What does you life say about what or who you love the most?

What would your life look like if you fell madly in love with God? Does it scare you to love God above all else? Why?

Q ~ Who of you by worrying can add a single hour to your life?
Luke 12:25

Reflection
Jesus talks about something we're all familiar with - *worry*. He places our anxious feelings in a context that involves God's goodness, involvement, and care. Jesus invites us to pay attention to creation, in this case - flowers and birds. He encourages us to notice how God takes care of them and then challenges us to let go of our worry and trust in God's power and generosity.

Discussion Prompts
On a scale from 1-10, how much do you "worry?"

What do you tend to worry about?

Prayer
Jesus, I'm worried about...   But my worrying doesn't actually change anything. It just makes me hard to be around. Give me the courage and the power to trust in you and to leave my worries behind. Help me to place my anxious feelings and thoughts in your hands and to be at peace with what I can actually influence and control. Grow me in my faith and help me to trust you more and more with every aspect of my life.

Digging Deeper
Consider your family of origin. Were you influenced/shaped by a family pattern of worrying?

How do you know when you are worrying? What are the telltale signs? How can others tell when you're feeling anxious?

Invite some friends over for tea. Invite everyone to talk about what they are worried about the most. Confess your worry and pray for each other. Read and discuss Luke 12:22-34.

Q ~ **Why do you entertain evil thoughts in your hearts?**
Matthew 9:4

Reflection
When Jesus asks this question, he talking with the "teachers of the law." He's not talking to unbelievers, but to the religious authorities. He uses a very colorful word "entertain" to describe what is happening.

Discussion Prompts
Consider the word "entertain." What images come to your mind when you think about this word?

Jesus associates "evil thoughts" not with the mind, but with the heart. What is the significance of this?

Prayer
Jesus, you see straight into my heart. Thank you telling me the truth about what you see there. Honestly, sometimes I know why I entertain evil thoughts and sometimes I don't. Help me to get at the root of why I've made a habit of feeding thoughts and desires that bring me down.

Digging Deeper
We are all sinners. We all entertain evil thoughts. What evil thoughts have you invited over for dinner? What sinful thoughts have you invited over for a slumber party?

What is it about your nature that makes you do this? Be honest and frank with yourself.

Imagine yourself serving drinks and appetizers to certain thoughts that you've invited over to your house. In your imagination, speak to these thoughts and inform them that the dinner will continue, but they are no longer welcome. Ask them to leave one by one. Be firm but kind. Read Philippians 4:8. Invite these guests over instead. Feed them and ask them to stay over for a slumber party.

Q ~ If you love those who love you, what reward will you get?
Matthew 5:46

Reflection
Jesus is talking about loving our enemies. Showing goodness and graciousness to those who don't give it back. When we love those who don't love us, we act just like God, who loved us while we were still sinners.

Discussion Prompts
What does the word "enemy" mean to you?

When is that last time you prayed for an enemy? Why or why not.

Prayer
Jesus, this is probably one of your most counter intuitive questions. My enemies are big jerks! But Lord, you loved me and showed me kindness when I wanted nothing to do with you. You came searching for me when I was lost, doing my own thing. You loved me when I didn't love you back... and now look at what you've done! Your gracious and faithful love drew me in and I had no choice but to surrender and to allow your love to turn my world upside down.

Digging Deeper
Pray for an enemy everyday this week. Did your feelings and attitudes change over time?

Allow yourself to feel the depths of your anger and hatred for your enemies. Pray for God to meet you in those feelings. Sit there for a while with Jesus.

Find a way to love someone who can't possibly love you back. Pay attention to this experience and write it down or tell a close friend about it.

Q ~ If I am telling the truth, why don't you believe me?
John 8:46

Reflection
Jesus asks a very powerful question in the midst of a dispute about truth and lies. Jesus insists that everything he says about himself, the kingdom, life and the Father is absolutely true. But those who are listening to him would rather believe lies.

Discussion Prompts
Do you really believe deep down that Jesus is telling the truth about everything? Why or why not?

Think about your life. What does your life/actions say about whether or not you truly believe Jesus?

Prayer
Jesus, I like to acknowledge you with my words, but then change nothing about my life. Sadly, because of the shape of my life, it seems as though I don't really believe you at all... or at least, I'm selective about what I believe. I have a lot of voices in my life telling me all kinds of things. Help me to see through the falsehood and to believe in ever deepening ways - your words.

Digging Deeper
What lies are you currently believing?

Who in your life speaks the truth to you? How do they go about doing it? Are you a truth speaker?

Read the Sermon on the Mount (Matthew 5-7). Read it believing that Jesus is telling the absolute and honest truth. Does this change anything for you?

Q ~ **Do you still have no faith?** *Mark 4:40*

Reflection
By this point in the gospel of Mark, Jesus has performed numerous miracles. The story in which this question comes is the story of Jesus calming the wind and the waves... perhaps his most powerful miracle to date. Jesus wonders what it will take for them to believe.

Discussion Prompts
Rate your faith on a scale from 1-10. Why that number?

Is faith hard or simple? Why?

Prayer
Jesus, you know I'm not there yet. But because of your grace, I'll keep growing in my faith every moment of everyday. It seems like the journey is always three steps forward and two steps back. Maybe I should be further along that I am. Your question causes me to take a good look at my faith and all the ways you've been faithful to me in the past.

Digging Deeper
Write down a list of how God has been faithful to you in the past. Do you see a pattern? How does this affect your current faith?

What is the biggest obstacle in your journey towards believing in Christ at ever deepening levels?

Imagine your fears as some sort of animal. See those animals threatening to attack and devour you. Then imagine Jesus stepping in and taming the wild beasts. See them submit and quiet down in the presence of Jesus. Listen to what Jesus wants to tell you about what has just happened.

Made in the USA
San Bernardino, CA
11 April 2016